THINKING AND WRITING ABOUT ART
UNDERSTANDING ART

LOIS FICHNER-RATHUS

PRENTICE HALL, Englewood Cliffs, NJ 07632

Editorial production/supervision and Interior Design: KRIS ANN E. CAPPELLUTI
Manufacturing buyers: HERB KLEIN AND PATRICE FRACCIO
Cover design: SUZANNE BEHNKE
Acquisitions editor: NORWELL THERIEN

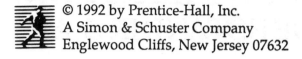

© 1992 by Prentice-Hall, Inc.
A Simon & Schuster Company
Englewood Cliffs, New Jersey 07632

Printed in the United States of America

10 9 8 7 6 5

ISBN 0-13-952565-3

Prentice-Hall International (UK) Limited, *London*
Prentice-Hall of Australia Pty. Limited, *Sydney*
Prentice-Hall Canada Inc., *Toronto*
Prentice-Hall Hispanoamericana, S.A., *Mexico*
Prentice-Hall of India Private Limited, *New Delhi*
Prentice-Hall of Japan, Inc., *Tokyo*
Simon & Schuster Asia Pte. Ltd., *Singapore*
Editora Prentice-Hall do Brasil, Ltda., *Rio de Janeiro*

PREFACE

When asked for their opinions on almost any subject, most students (and most of the rest of us) go on for what seems to be an eternity. Yet when asked to think and write about the visual arts, many students are suddenly dumbstruck. There are reasons for this. For one thing, most students are not as familiar with art and the vocabulary used to think and talk about art as they are with many other areas of life. For another, art may seem particularly exotic or removed from everyday experience, so students may be afraid that they will put their feet into their mouths when they attempt to express themselves. But there is still another reason: many students simply have not received adequate training and practice in critical thinking and writing. For these students, problems in thinking and writing about art are generalizations from more basic difficulties in evaluating and expressing experiences.

I wrote this supplement to my textbook, *Understanding Art*, primarily to stimulate students to think and write about art. In doing so, however, this supplement will also help colleges, professors, and students meet two widespread pedagogical objectives:

1. Critical thinking,
2. Writing across the curriculum.

INTRODUCTION

Throughout high school and college, many students have the feeling that compositions and papers are part of the price they have to pay to get a diploma and, eventually, a decent job. But they do not see writing as something valuable in itself.

The fact is that writing is essential, not only in college but also in most professional careers. Business executives need to be able to communicate their ideas through writing. Marketing plans, advertising copy, and proposals for new products must all be fleshed out in words and sentences. Very few lawyers put on courtroom shows like the fabled Perry Mason; most lawyers spend far more time writing contracts and persuasive letters. Technicians, engineers, and scientists have to be able to write precise reports. Think of all the writing that goes into directions for using a stove or a VCR. Consider the detailed writing that is found in armed forces weapons manuals. Engineers and scientists also write technical articles for journals; they review the research in their fields and report on their own experiments. They have to be able to write clearly enough so that other people can follow their directions and arrive at the same results accurately and safely. Doctors, psychologists, counselors, nurses, and dental hygienists must be able to write up reports describing the problems and progress of their patients and clients. Managers of fast-food restaurants write evaluations of employees. Everyone writes business letters of one kind or another—or is inconvenienced if he or she cannot.

So writing skills are not for college only. Writing skills are not just the province of English teachers, poets, novelists, and journalists. They are for everyone who is receiving an education and contemplating a career.

KINDS OF WRITING

There are many kinds of writing. Writing can be broken down into fiction (imaginary happenings, such as short stories, plays, and novels) and nonfiction (such as directions for assembling machines, essays, theme papers, and term papers). The writing of fiction is usually taught in creative writing courses, although fiction is sometimes assigned in freshman composition classes. Students need not be good at writing fiction to get by in college—unless they're making up excuses as to why they are late with their assignments! By and large, however, college students are required to show or develop some skill at writing nonfiction.

The kinds of nonfiction required of

college students are mostly essay answers on tests, theme papers, and term papers. Here I focus on theme papers and term papers. A theme is a relatively short paper and is the most common type of paper assigned in courses like freshman composition. There are different kinds of themes, including argumentative, descriptive, and expository.

The aim of the *argumentative theme* is to persuade the reader to adopt a certain point of view. Papers intended to convince the reader that Lady Macbeth was motivated by infertility or that the greenhouse effect will eventually cause persistent droughts in the midwestern breadbasket are argumentative.

A *descriptive theme* paints in words persons, places, or ideas. The infamous "What I Did on My Summer Vacation" theme is basically descriptive. If you have poetic urges, it is usually best to give vent to them in descriptive themes. Expository themes are explanatory in nature. They are concrete and logically developed.

Expository themes apply to the instructions in your cookbook for concocting guacamole and to laboratory reports. Each discipline (art, biology, physics, psychology, etc.) has its own way of doing things, its own traditions, but they also have some things in common: Explanations are kept as brief and precise as possible. Usually, you explain what you set out to do, why you set out to do it, what you actually did, what you found out, and, sometimes, the implications of what you discovered.

Term papers differ from theme papers in a number of ways. One is length. The paper is called a term paper because it is supposed to take a good part of the term to write it, or because it is intended to reflect what you have learned during the term. Also, term papers usually require references to books and articles on their subjects. That means that research is also required. If the research base of your term paper is to be solid, it could take you longer to do the research, including taking notes, than to write the paper itself.

CRITICAL THINKING

In the fifteenth century it was widely believed that the Earth was flat. In the sixteenth century it was widely believed that the sun revolved around the Earth. It seems that widely held beliefs are invariably replaced by other widely held beliefs in the fullness of time. It is the hallmark of an educated person to remain skeptical of accepted views and to regard even the most popular beliefs as working assumptions. In the twentieth century, most astronomers widely believe that the universe began with a "big bang" and has been expanding ever since. It is fascinating to speculate on what views will replace these beliefs tomorrow.

In order to help students evaluate claims, arguments, and widely held beliefs, most colleges today encourage *critical thinking*. Critical thinking has many meanings. On one level, it means taking nothing for granted. It means not believing things just because they are in print or because they were uttered by authority figures or celebrities. It means not necessarily believing that a painting is a good painting, or a bad painting, because a critic says so. On another level, critical thinking refers to a process of thoughtfully analyzing and probing the questions, statements, and arguments of others. It means examining definitions of terms, examining the premises or assumptions behind arguments, and then scrutinizing the logic with which arguments are developed.

The emphasis on critical thinking reflects the widespread belief that your college education is intended to do more than provide you with a data bank of useful knowledge. It is also meant to provide you with intellectual tools that allow you to learn from and analyze information independently. With these tools, you can continue to educate yourself for the rest of your life.

Colleges nurture academic freedom, so few professors require (or want) students to share and express their own beliefs. By and large, professors are more concerned that students learn how to question and critically examine their subjects, the points of view of other people, and even their own convictions and values. (Your instructor might find your statement "Abstract art is bogus!" to represent something less than a high level of critical thinking.) This does not mean that professors insist that students change their beliefs, either. It does mean, however, that professors usually ask students to *support* the views they express in class and in their writing. If students' definitions of terms are muddy, if their premises are shaky, or if their arguments are illogical, professors may encourage other students to challenge them or may personally point out the fallacies in their arguments. Most professors want students to learn to recognize the premises of their arguments, to consider whether they really accept these premises, and to understand whether or not they draw logical conclusions from them.

The following section outlines some of the principles of critical thinking.

Some Features of Critical Thinking

1. Be skeptical. Politicians and advertisers strive to convince you of their points of view. Even the information reported in textbooks may take a certain slant. Have the attitude that you will accept nothing as true until you have personally examined the evidence. But also have the idea that your own attitudes and beliefs may be superficial or unfounded until you have examined them critically.

2. Examine definitions of terms. Some statements are true when a term is defined in one way but not another. Consider the statement, "Robert Mapplethorpe's photographs of men engaged in homosexual activity are obscene." The statement is true if homosexuality is considered obscene, or if depictions of sexual activity are considered obscene. But the Supreme Court has recently held that obscenity is to be judged in terms of community standards, and the case against a Cincinnati gallery that had shown the works of Mapplethorpe was dismissed.

3. Examine the assumptions or premises of arguments. Consider the statements "The greatest art was produced during the Renaissance," "There is a clear distinction between crafts and fine arts," etc.

4. Be cautious in drawing conclusions from evidence. It may be easier to point a camera at a subject than to paint the subject, but does this "evidence" mean that photography is not an exacting or fine art form?

5. Do not oversimplify. Students tend to make many simplistic statements, such as "Pop art is a rip-off" and "Conceptual artists are only out for the money." There is more to Pop art and Conceptual art than meets these student's eyes, at least, and students need to be open to new experiences and new ways of evaluating experience. What is wrong with the following statement?: "Anyone can paint an abstract picture."

6. Do not overgeneralize. Consider the statement "Abstract art is less difficult to execute than realistic art." Unless you have truly evaluated *all* abstract art and *all* realistic art, you are about to sink into a quagmire of your own making. Also, can you equate level of difficulty, as it refers to time spent or materials utilized, with quality in a work of art? If you wish to explore the comparative difficulties of executing various works of art, focus in on a controllable number of concrete examples that you have some hope of handling. How may the statement "Renaissance art is superior to contemporary art" get you into similar trouble?

7. Apply critical thinking to all areas of life. A skeptical attitude and a demand for evidence are not simply academic exercises that serve in courses on art and other college

subjects. They are of value in all areas of life. Be skeptical when you are bombarded by television commercials, when political causes try to sweep you in, when you see the latest cover story about UFOs on the tabloids at the supermarket. How many times have you heard the claim, "Studies have shown that . . ."? Perhaps it sounds convincing, but ask yourself, Who ran the studies? Were the researchers neutral scientists or biased toward obtaining certain results? Were there controls? Blinds? Who were the subjects? Were they assigned to groups at random?

As noted by the educator Robert M. Hutchins, "The object of education is to prepare the young to educate themselves throughout their lives." One of the primary ways of educating yourself is through critical thinking.

Recognizing Common Fallacies in Arguments

Another aspect of critical thinking is learning to recognize the fallacies in other people's claims and arguments. Consider the following examples.

1. Arguments Directed to the Person (*Argumentum ad Hominem*): In 1989 the Supreme Court ruled that the principle of freedom of speech gives people the right to burn the American flag as a form of political protest, setting off divisive arguments and a call for an amendment to the Constitution that would protect the flag. The lawyer who won the Supreme Court case was William Kunstler, who had years earlier defended many protesters against the Vietnam War. Some opponents of the Supreme Court decision on flag burning directed their wrath against Kunstler, arguing that he was the "radical, leftist" lawyer who had defended the "Chicago Seven," etc. This is an *ad hominem* argument.

Kunstler as a person is irrelevant, however; the critical issue involves the interpretation of the U. S. Constitution.

2. Arguments Employing Force (*Argumentum ad Baculum*): Galileo invented the telescope in the seventeenth century and discovered that the Earth revolved around the sun, rather than vice versa. However, the church had taught that the Earth was at the center of the universe. Galileo was condemned for heresy and warned that he would be burned to death if he did not confess the error of his ways. Galileo apparently agreed with Shakespeare that "The better part of valour is discretion"[1] and recanted his views, but the facts of course are as they are. Social approval and, at the opposite extreme, threats of violence do not make arguments correct or incorrect.

3. Appeals to Authority (*Argumentum ad Verecundiam*): How many times have you heard arguments to the effect, "Well, my mother/teacher/ minister says this is true, and I think that he/she knows more about it than you do"? Appeals to authority can be persuasive or infuriating, depending on whether or not you agree with them; however, it matters not *who* makes an assertion. An argument is either true or false on its own merits. Consider the evidence presented in arguments, not the person making the argument, no matter how exalted.

4. Appeals to Popularity (*Argumentum ad Populum*): The appeal to popularity is cousin to the appeal to authority. It is perhaps best (and most often) illustrated by the TV commercial or newspaper advertisement. If Bill Cosby advertises Jello, for example, can Jello be bad? Bill Cosby is a highly popular public figure. (His television role of *Doctor* Huxtable also makes him appear to be an authority figure.) The people making the

---

[1] *King Henry IV, Part I*, Act v, Scene iv.

pitches in TV commercials are usually very popular—either because they are good looking or because they are celebrities. Again, critically evaluate the evidence being presented and ignore the appeal of the person making the pitch.

The argument that you should do something or believe something because "everyone's doing it" is another type of appeal to popularity—one that gets some people involved in activities they later regret. A majority vote may pass a bill in the legislature, but it does not mean that the arguments in favor of the bill are correct—even if the vote is unanimous.

Similarly, abstract art is not good art because thousands of artists work in the style. Specific works of abstract art succeed or fail on their own merits, and the standards used to judge them should not be appeals to authority or popularity. The student who says that a work is good or bad because the instructor says so knows nothing of the work.

In sum, be skeptical of claims and arguments. Critically examine the evidence presented rather than focusing on the authority, force, or appeal of the people making the argument.

GUIDELINES FOR ANALYZING WORKS OF ART

The analysis of a work of art has many aspects, including description, interpretation, even criticism. The description will consist of first, what is there, and second, how it has been rendered (questions of style). Interpretation of a work revolves around other things—the sociopolitical currents of the era in which it was created, iconographic (symbolic, thematic) issues, even its relationship to other works. Criticism refers to judging the work's aesthetic qualities and the factors that contribute to or detract from them.

There is no single way to analyze a work of art—no single set of standards by which to make judgments, no single outline according to which to present your thoughts. The following guidelines are intended to summarize the types of issues critics usually address, and to help you think about the work of art before you so that you truly perceive it. If you are already well-schooled in thinking and writing about art, feel free to move beyond the guidelines and go off on your own. If you are a novice, however, it would be a good idea to consider each and every guideline. It might even be worthwhile to have the attitude that no guideline is to be ignored, unless you have a convincing reason for doing so.

Running through the guidelines can be somewhat mechanical, so you may also wish, at the start, to try something more spontaneous. Before going through the guidelines, why not stand in front of the work and consider your first impressions? What strikes you about it? Something about the subject matter? The colors? The materials? What hits you first? It may be that by "letting yourself go," you will hit upon an interesting way to approach your analysis, even a novel insight or two. After all, being new to the game can have some advantages as well as disadvantages. You may bring a "fresh eye" to the consideration of venerable works. To some degree, in other words, it may be good to trust your instincts. *This is not to excuse the eventual consideration of all of the guidelines and the piecing together of all of your impressions, but it is to suggest that newcomers often have worthwhile perceptions and thoughts to offer.*

In analyzing works of art, I recommend that you pay attention to factors such as their setting or site, their materials and techniques, their plastic elements (line, light, color, and so forth), their composition, their content, their place in history, and—guess what—their title. I am not suggesting that you write an extended outline with full sentences. Rather, let some form of inspiration—some immediate response to the work—be your starting point. Write down what you can—what you see, what you feel. Then run through the guidelines. Consider everything, but ultimately pick and choose. When you pull together your analysis of the work, use your intelligence to integrate the shards of information that comprise the more meaningful guidelines into a unified whole.

Analyzing the Setting: Where Is the Work?

Where are you viewing the work? Is it a painting on a wall in a museum or gallery? Are you kept away from it or allowed to touch it or otherwise relate to it? (In one museum I was allowed to walk into Lucas Samaras's *Mirrored Room*; in another, I had to crane my neck to steal glances within—to very different effects.)

Where was the work originally displayed or seen? Was it intended to be viewed by itself, or in the midst of other works? What effect do you imagine the original site had on the work? How about its present location? For example, what does it add or signify that a sculpture was once a part of a pediment of the Parthenon? Or that Michelangelo's painting of the creation of Adam rises high above us in the ceiling of the Sistine Chapel?

If a sculpture, is the work situated aesthetically within a building, plaza, or garden? Does it complement the greenery or architecture or neighboring works in the area? Does it offer an interesting counterpoint? Is it dwarfed by its surroundings, or overwhelm them? If a building, how is it integrated with its site? Is a contemporary house oblivious to its wooded site, or does it invite the foliage within? Is an office building "plunked down in the middle of nowhere"? Is a building congruous in terms of style and scale with neighboring buildings? If not, does the incongruity enhance or detract from the appearance of the building and, indeed, the neighborhood?

Analyzing the Materials and Techniques: What Is It Made Of?

"Every material has its own individual qualities," noted sculptor Henry Moore. What is the work made of—charcoal, paint, paper, canvas, steel, glass? Sticks and stones? A combination of several of these?

What are the qualities of the materials employed? Do the materials seem to be appropriate to the medium and the subject matter of the work? Are the materials the norm for the era in which the work was created, or are they innovative? What impression is made by the materials? Does it seem to you that the application of materials is relatively unremarkable, or does it seem that the artist was "making a statement" through them?

Moore also remarked that "Stone . . . is hard and should not be falsified to look like soft flesh." Does the artist "falsify" his or her material(s) to create novel impressions? How?

In the case of a building, what are the structural properties of the materials? At the time the building was created, how new was the technology needed to create the material? What is the effect of the materials on climate control? What alternatives did the architect have available? How do the materials chosen contribute to the aesthetic and practical attributes of the work? Are the materials consonant with (or perhaps gathered from) the site?

How has the artist worked the materials? If oil paint, for example, are there small, even brushstrokes (brushstrokes that downplay the "personal signature" of the artist), or are there broad swaths and generous use of impasto? To what effect? Is the working of the materials traditional for the era and the medium, or is it innovative? In the case of architecture, how are the materials assembled into buildings or structures? Is the technique innovative? If so, how?

Another aspect of the materials and techniques employed is found in the *condition* of the work. Describe the surface. Is the work relatively new and unscathed, or time-worn or damaged? Is it an ancient work in remarkable condition, or a contemporary piece that seems to be falling apart? Has the work been restored? (Can you tell if it has?) Is the work complete, or are you observing only fragments of the original? In the case of an ancient sculpture, are you looking at the original or a copy? Though it may appear a pristine white, was it ever painted? Has its site changed (from temple to museum)? To what effect? If you are viewing architecture, has it been rebuilt? Renovated? Has its site changed—did it once stand alone where it is now nestled among other buildings? To what effect?

Analyzing the Use of the Plastic Elements of Art

The so-called plastic elements of the visual arts include line, shape, light, color, texture, mass, space, and actual and implied time and motion. These elements are arranged or organized according to principles of unity, balance, and rhythm, among others, to form what is known as a composition. The content of the work refers to the images within it—perhaps a human figure, a landscape, geometric shapes, or perhaps simply lines and textures.

LINE

How is line used to depict the subject matter? As in some abstract works, are lines themselves the subject matter? Are lines thin and delicate, or broad and brusque? Are long, single lines used to enclose space, to outline or suggest forms, or is the work composed of myriad tiny lines? Are lines used to model forms or to create impressions of textures? Is the composition created by a discrete number of bold lines, or is it built around a more subtle use of line?

Does the use of line seem traditional for the medium, the area, and the subject matter, or is it innovative? Do the lines tend to be thick or thin, long or short, smooth or jagged? Is their character expressive?

SHAPE

We tend to organize lines into figure-ground relationships. We tend to perceive shapes as figures against backgrounds. We also tend to integrate parts into meaningful wholes, even when there are gaps in sensory information. Shape can be communicated by dominant lines that enclose specific areas in a work. Shape can also be communicated through patches of color or texture. In three-dimensional works such as sculpture and architecture, shape is

discerned when the work is viewed against its environment. The edges, colors, and textures of the work give it shape against the background.

How are shapes created or communicated in the work? What is their relationship to one another and the whole? Are the shapes predominant in the composition or subservient to it?

LIGHT

How important is light to the composition? Is it uniform, or is a spot-lighting effect employed? Can you identify a light source? If two-dimensional, like a painting, is it in the work, or is the light source outside of the work? Is it a natural light, or is it unnatural and distorting? Is chiaroscuro employed—that is, do subtle gradations of light and shade create a sense of three-dimensionality on the two-dimensional surface? How do gradations in light give rise to a sense of texture? Do severe contrasts create plunges in depth or heighten the emotional impact of the work?

If a three-dimensional work, how do changing lighting conditions affect the perception of the work? How does the depth of carving (shallow or deep) work with light to create the illusion of reality? What happens to light or lighting as well as surface details as you walk around or through the work? How does the play of light or the use of dramatic contrasts affect your response to the work?

COLOR

Describe the palette the artist employs. Is it light or dark? Is it monochromatic or polychromatic? Are the colors highly saturated (pure)? Are they analogous or complementary? Are they predominant over the other plastic elements or subservient to them?

Are the colors true to nature? If not, how do they differ? What is the effect of the departure from nature? In some works, as in color-field paintings, color seems very much to be the subject of the work. What is the role of color in the work you are observing? Does the color seem to be subordinated to the forms and the content of the work, or does the color dramatically create its own form or content? How does the color affect your emotional response to the work? What does the use of color suggest about the intentions and emotions of the artist? Does the use of color appear to contribute to or detract from the aesthetic aspects of the work? Why? Is the use of color innovative? Are the materials used to create the color innovative?

TEXTURE

The texture of a work is its surface character as experienced primarily through the sense of touch. Artists often use line, color, and other plastic elements to create the illusion of textures in works of different media. When the surfaces of objects, real or imagined, are depicted in such a way as to create the illusion of actual textures (fur, feathers, marble, even globs of goo), the composition is said to possess implied texture. Sculptors and architects, of course, deal with actual textures in their media—stone, wood, plaster, clay, steel, and many other materials. Painters too have experimented with textural materials in their canvases in lieu of traditional pigments.

What are the implied or actual textures of the work? How are the textures created? Through line? Through color and brushwork? Are the textures true to their subject or at odds with it? What kind of emotional response does the texture elicit?

What kind of surface or facing does the work have? If it is a painting, is it varnished? (Have protective coatings been removed or replaced in a restoration process?) Are the brushstrokes smooth and invisible (does the surface of the canvas have a mirror-like finish?) or are they thick or crusty? How would you define the strokes—daubs of paint, dots of paint, block-like strokes? Do you think the artist used a brush? A palette knife? The wooden end of the brush? Do you think the paint was dripped, spilled, spattered? Does it sit on the canvas or literally stain it?

If the work is a sculpture, what tools do you imagine the artist used to create the surface textures and details? Is the surface smooth or coarse, or a combination of the two? Has the surface become pitted, discolored, or otherwise worn with time? Are any sections of the surface in their original condition? What of the facade of a building? Is their a unity to the textures? A diversity? Do the textures seem to complement the dimensions of the building? Its relationship to the site, to the ground, to the sky?

MASS

Mass refers to bulk, size, or magnitude. In most two-dimensional works of art, the mass of a depicted object is implied; in most sculpture or architecture the mass is actual. I say "most" because sometimes the artist will create a disconcerting effect in a painting by, let's say, depicting a massive object that defies gravity; in spite of its actual mass, a glass-faced skyscraper can have an ethereal, or weightless quality.

How is mass conveyed, implied, reinforced, or denied in the work before you? Describe the masses that compose the image. Are they shapes, forms, blocks or areas of color? How do they relate to one another and the whole? Do they lend stability to the work? Do they threaten to throw the whole out of whack? In a sculpture or a building, how does its mass or massiveness relate to its aesthetic character?

SPACE

A large part of the history of painting has revolved around creating the illusion of actual, three-dimensional space on a two-dimensional surface. All types of perspective (atmospheric, herringbone, linear, etc.) were developed to give viewers the sense that the picture frame was comparable to the window frame: You could look through it, forever and ever, into the distance. Techniques for foreshortening were developed to relate figures and objects to this space.

A large part of the history of modern painting, curiously, has revolved around the cancellation of that illusionistic space and the assertion of the reality, or concrete nature, of the canvas's two-dimensional surface: No more "window frame," no more foreshortening, no more subtle and realistic modeling of objects. The representation of space, or the deliberate destruction of it, however, are not the artist's only options. Consider the artist who creates a "sense" of space, through the manipulation of plastic elements in an abstract composition. (Jackson Pollock's vast drip compositions have been, for example, likened to sprawling, if chaotic, landscapes.) Does the artist before you recreate realistic space? Cancel any suggestion of depth? Construct an analogy for space in abstract terms? If you are looking at a sculpture, or perhaps a building, how does the artist or architect integrate or interrupt the space surrounding the work into its overall composition? Does the work create a sense of space that reflects an era (is it sort-of flat, like a Byzantine Mosaic, or deep, like a Baroque ceiling painting)? Is the work "modern" in that there is a flattening of pictorial depth? How is the illusion of depth created? How is the suggestion of depth suppressed? Is perspective used? How so?

Three-dimensional works such as sculptures and buildings have real volume and exist in (and/or enclose) real space. What are the major volumes of a sculpture? As you walk around it, how do the volumes relate to one another? Is the sculpture "dense," or does space flow through it? To what effect? (Sculptor Henry Moore commented that the open spaces "within" sculptures—holes—can have as much "shape-meaning" as the solid masses.) What kinds of spaces are enclosed by a building? Are these spaces suggested by the exterior or are they a surprise? Are these spaces aesthetic or are they the "price" that the architect pays to achieve some unusual exterior effect?

TIME AND MOTION

Artists have sought to represent movement and the passage of time in essentially static media such as drawing, painting, still photography, and sculpture. Only recently have art forms been developed that involve actual time and actual movement, such as kinetic sculpture and motion pictures.

Does the artist *imply* motion and/or the passage of time in the work? How? Are frames used to advance a narrative? Are several parts of a story incorporated into a single work? Do lines, echoing shapes, or color reverberations suggest fluttering or other types of motion? Does the posture of a figure—as in Bernini's *David*—suggest stopped action? Is a single moment isolated in time? Can you imagine the story or the action before and after the single moment as it is portrayed?

Analyzing the Composition: How Does It Go Together?

How is the work composed? How are the pieces put together? Principles such as proportion and scale, unity, balance, and rhythm are used in the creation of compositions.

PROPORTION AND SCALE

How do the parts of the work, or the images within, relate to one another and to the whole? Are any principles at work, such as the classical Greek canon of proportions, which had been used to perfect the human figure? Are the proportions realistic or distorted? If distorted, what is the emotional effect?

What is the size of the work? Is it smaller or larger than "life-size"? What is its size in relation to people? Does the artist cram a wealth of intricate detail within a confined space, or overwhelm you with enormity? If you have seen the work previously in class or in your book, can you comment on the difference between being in the actual presence of the work and seeing it in a slide or as a textbook illustration? Are you pleasantly surprised by the scale or are you disappointed? If you are looking at architecture, is the size of the building or structure an important element in its aesthetic impact?

UNITY

Unity is oneness or wholeness. A work of art achieves unity when its parts seem integral to the success of a composition. Unity can also be achieved through sameness, or the repetition of like or similar elements throughout a composition (as in a pattern, for example). The *Parthenon* of ancient Greece is a fine example of both methods used to achieve unity. Artists also sometimes work with the principle of variety within unity, creating compositional interest through marked contrasts. Jennifer Bartlett's *2 Priory Walk* is a good example of this principle. Does the work achieve a sense of unity? (Or why does it not do so?) How? Do you feel that you can switch around any of the composition's components and have an equally successful work? In what ways do unity or variety within unity create visual interest?

BALANCE

Balance in a work can be achieved through the manipulation of any number of plastic elements and design principles: shape, color, mass, even scale. Balance can be symmetrical (objects on the left match objects on the right), or asymmetrical (objects on the left differ from objects on the right, but they have equal "weight" or emphasis on the whole). Is there a sense of balance in the work? What type of balance? Which plastic elements are used to achieve it? If the work is not in balance (as when a portion of a three-dimensional work is cantilevered), where is the center of gravity? Do compensating elements create a visual balance?

RHYTHM

Rhythm in a work of art or architecture implies repetition and orderly progression, echoing shapes or lines. These techniques and elements are employed to different effect: logic, order and quietude (as in a Gothic cathedral vault), or perhaps, banality and monotony (as in Warhol's *Coca-Cola Bottles*). Are there natural rhythms or orderly progressions that contribute to the aesthetic features of the work? What is the emotional effect of these rhythms? The symbolism?

Analyzing Levels of Content: What Is There? (And What Else?)

The content of a work of art is everything that is contained within it. Content refers not only to elements and composition, but also to images, subject matter and their underlying meanings or themes.

SUBJECT MATTER

The subject matter of a work is the *what* of the work. What are the images in the work? *What* is painted, drawn, carved, photographed? Do we see people? Landscape? Abstract, biomorphic forms? Color fields? An amphitheater or house in Levittown? Is Judith decapitating Holofernes? Is a family relaxing on a Harlem rooftop in summer?

ICONOGRAPHY

Iconography is the systematic investigation of subject matter; it concerns the identification, description, categorization, and explanation of themes and symbols found in a work of art. The interpretation of subject matter—the actual meaning of the work of art—in light of its symbolism, as well as its cultural and historical background—is called *iconology*. Bronzino's *Venus, Cupid, Folly, and Time (The Exposure of Luxury)* and Jan Van Eyck's *Giovanni Arnolfini and His Bride* are classic examples of works in which there is much more than meets the eye. The Bronzino painting weaves an intricate allegory, laden with many symbols. In the van Eyck, the items scattered about are invested with symbolism relevant to the occasion. The dog symbolizes fidelity. The oranges may symbolize victory over death. The finial on the bedpost is an image of St. Margaret, the patroness of childbirth. Around her waist is a small whisk broom, a symbol of domesticity.

What do the images in the work symbolize? Are the symbols common knowledge today (such as a lily symbolizing purity, or a lion symbolizing courage and strength), or are they obscure? Do they hold the key to the interpretation of the work, or are they "fluff?" Is it possible to understand or enjoy the work without knowledge of the symbolism, or does ignorance of the symbolic meaning compromise full appreciation of the work?

Thinking about content also extends to considering the larger context of the work. You may, for example, wish to consider the era and sociopolitical climate in which the work was created. Who else was around at the time the work was created? Which writers, composers, scientists, philosophers? Are there any stylistic similarities between the way the visual artist approached his or her medium and the message and the ways in which contemporaries in other disciplines approached their productions? Can you compare Vivaldi and Bernini? Beethoven and Delacroix? Did Euclid have an influence on Greek architecture? Is Non-Euclidian geometry responsible for cubism? Art history is a truly interdisciplinary subject.

Referring to the History of Art: Where Does the Work Belong?

Knowledge of the history of art allows us to appreciate the evolution of styles, the contrasts or conflicts among artists from various schools and movements, the social and political influences on artists, and the role of art and artist within society.

Assume that the work you are analyzing contains one or more human figures. What can knowledge of the history of art add to your understanding of the way in which the figures are depicted? They may be true to nature or they may be distorted. What movements have distorted the human figure? Why? Can we always equate truth to reality with artistic skill? Which movements or cultures put a premium on realism? For which was (is) realism limiting or meaningless? Did (does) the work represent brave innovations or follow established taste? How does knowledge of the era in which the work was created contribute to your analysis? If you have

never seen the work before (or anything else like it), can you draw parallels to works with which you are familiar in order to attempt to place it within some stylistic context? Do not concern yourself if you are wrong; even if what you are looking at is far afield from the work in your mind that you think it resembles, the comparison will still be interesting. Take a look at the date of the work and its country of origin. Conversely, you may find that the work is not at all like others you know of the same period and place. How is it different? The nature of a work of art can be linked to the artist's personal history as well as to the era and sociopolitical climate in which it was created. The value of recognizing that the works of van Gogh and Gauguin follow Impressionism and precede Expressionism may seem obvious enough (after you have taken a course in art!). But can we better understand why these works look the way they do by becoming aware of the personal difficulties that these artists experienced? Is there a value to knowing about the conflict between Michelangelo and Pope Julius II when we stand beneath the ceiling of the Sistine Chapel?

Considering the Title: Would a Work By Any Other Name Be as Visually Appealing?

Great clues to artist's intentions are found in titles. Sometimes. What is the title of the work? What does the title suggest about the content of the work? Sometimes the title is very telling. Consider two works by Mondrian discussed in Chapter 2: One is entitled *Composition in Red, Blue, and Yellow*, the other *Broadway Boogie-Woogie*. The titles suggest that the former may be non-objective, whereas the latter is likely to be an abstraction of the vibrant grid of Manhattan. But beware: Artists (and even others—their friends and family, maybe a critic who visited the studio) have come up with titles for works only after they were executed. Such post-production nametags may or may not have anything to do with the content, or the original thought that gave rise to it.

Then, too, many, many works are titled *Untitled*—just like that overly worked Professor Staff, whom you find in the course listings each term. Do not despair when a work is untitled, however. The lack of a title may reflect the artist's refusal to pigeonhole the work, or it may mean that the artist is inviting the viewer to make his or her own interpretations. If so, that, too, is useful information.

GUIDELINES FOR GOOD WRITING

Just as no two people are exactly alike (even identical twins have their own private thoughts), no two people write exactly alike. Good writing takes many forms. Some people use slang very well; others fare better when they take a more formal approach. Some writers show strong organizational skills; others have a fine poetic touch and the ability to create vivid images through words. Yet, there are a number of guidelines that hold true for most of us most of the time.

Complete the Assignment

It may not matter how your intelligence and sophistication shine through or how your prose sparkles if you do not follow instructions and carry out the assignment. Make sure that you understand the instructions. If your professor asks for a looking assignment, a paper on a work of art in a museum or a building on campus, make sure that you understand what the professor means by *looking assignment*. If class discussion of the requirements does not create a clear picture for you, ask for examples in the professor's office. You can also ask the instructor to show you one or more models (pieces of writing) that fulfill the assignment.

Write for Your Audience

If you are writing a children's story, keep the vocabulary simple and the sentences short. If you are writing an argumentative theme to persuade people that music videos

defile cinematographic techniques, be prepared to use the proper technical vocabulary and to distinguish carefully between facts and opinions.

Write Clearly and Simply

Most good writing is reasonably easy to read. Don't have the idea that intelligent writing has to be hard to follow, like a Henry James novel or a Shakespearean play. Unless your assignment is to write a Victorian novel or an Elizabethan play, don't try to manufacture an intricate style or several layers of meaning.

Be Willing to Make Mistakes

No college student (or any other person) is a perfect writer. Everyone makes mistakes. If you didn't make mistakes, you wouldn't need an education, would you?

The point is to learn from your errors. When some aspect of a writing exercise is marked as poor, or wrong, make sure that you understand why. If you do not, you may repeat the mistake.

Keep a Notebook or a Journal

Creative writers, journalism students, and English majors are encouraged to keep notebooks to jot down important thoughts as they occur. Sometimes they record the events around them—the heavy sky that threatens to burst into a storm or the suspended animation of a frozen January hillside; at other times they record their inmost thoughts and feelings. You may wish to keep a journal in which you note your responses to works of art, crafts, buildings, photographs (in magazines, for example—why not cut things out and make a scrapbook of interesting photos, but not from library books and periodicals, guys), films, or TV shows.

Determine Length Intelligently: How Long Should a Paper Be?

Students are perpetually concerned about how long a paper should be. The correct answer is simple in principle, but it still leaves many students dissatisfied. Generally speaking, the right number of words is the minimal number it takes to do the job. Put another way: Everything else being equal, a briefer paper is better than a longer paper.

If you're not sure how long a paper should be, ask the professor or check out previous papers that earned high grades. If the professor is not specific about numbers of words or pages, perhaps he or she can give you an impression of how long it should take to write the paper. Is it a paper that you ought to be able to write in one afternoon or evening? Perhaps that would be two to five pages long (typed, double-spaced). Is it a term paper that requires a few days of library work and a few more days of writing? If so, 20 to 30 typewritten, double-spaced pages (including footnotes and bibliography) might be in order.

In any case, if the instructor specifies the number of pages for an assignment, be sure to comply. Failure to do so, even by a few pages in one direction or another, can result in a lower grade.

Avoid Plagiarism

> I found your essay to be good and original. However, the part that was original was not good and the part that was good was not original.
>
> —Samuel Johnson

Plagiarism derives from the Latin *plagiarius*, which roughly translates as "kidnapper" in English. Plagiarism is literary theft—the stealing of another person's ideas or words and passing them off as your own.

Let's be honest. Some students intentionally steal the work of others. They pass off a paper that was written by a fraternity brother eight years ago as their own, or they copy passages of books verbatim. And students aren't the only ones; news reports now and then carry charges of plagiarism by film script writers, or even politicians. I have even known architecture students to steal designs from magazines. Other

students plagiarize inadvertently, however. The penalties for plagiarism can be severe. Failing the paper is a minimal penalty; plagiarizers can also fail the course. Now and then, students are pressured to withdraw from college as a result of plagiarism. Stiff penalties seem appropriate for purposeful plagiarism. It is a pity to suffer them, however, for accidental plagiarism.

Professors may not be able to determine whether students have adapted or copied the papers of other students. It is relatively easy, however, for professors to discern passages that have been taken whole from books or articles. The passage may show a level of literary sophistication that exceeds that of the great majority of students. There may be a cogent recounting of facts that could be created only by an expert in the field. There may also be obvious inconsistencies in the paper: The student's own writing may struggle for clarity, while pilfered passages shine through.

The following guidelines will enable you to avoid the pitfalls and penalties of plagiarism.

1. When you mention other people's ideas or theories, attribute the ideas to their proper source. Write, for example,

    > Although the Renaissance is said to have been characterized by a rebirth of the classical, Vasari[2] notes that we find little in the spirit and form of the work of Donatello that we can consider classical. There is also scant written record, according to Vasari, to support the idea that Leonardo was highly versed in the art of Greece and Rome.

---

[2]Here you footnote the source according to your professor's instructions or style sheet. You usually include the name of the author (or authors), the title of the work, and other information as specified. For books, you also usually include the name of the publisher and the city and date of publication. For magazine and journal articles, you also usually include the name of the magazine or journal, the volume number, the issue number, and the page numbers.

2. When you use other people's words, either place them in quotation marks or indent the material. Let length be your guide. When a passage runs from a few words to about four lines, use quotation marks. If a passage runs to five or more lines, indent the material similarly to the way I indented the preceding material on Renaissance art and Vasari.[3] Place your footnote, however, at the end of the quoted material. Whether you use quotation marks or indent, note the source of the material, including the page or pages on which it is found.

3. You can usually use a brief string (say two or three words) of your source's writing without using quotation marks. But use quotation marks if one of the words is a technical term or shows a fine literary turn of phrase—something you would not have arrived at on your own.

4. Hold on to the outline (if you used one) and the working drafts of your paper. If you are falsely accused of plagiarism, you can trace the development of your ideas and your phrasing.

Pick a Topic

You say there is nothing to write about. Then write to me that there is nothing to write about.

Pliny the Younger

There are no dull subjects. There are only dull writers.

H. L. Mencken

Sometimes professors assign concrete topics, such as a reaction to a piece of writing. Or they provide a list of concrete topics, from which the student must choose. Sometimes professors purposefully leave topics wide open. Professors may also assign a paper on some aspect of a topic, which tends to leave the decision pretty much to the student.

There are no hard-and-fast rules to picking a topic. By and large, however, writers—including college students—tend to be at their best on subjects with which they are familiar. Let us consider some motives for picking topics and ways to make them manageable.

WRITE ABOUT THINGS YOU KNOW ABOUT

The first novels of writers tend to be autobiographic. This is true, in part, because writers seek ways of expressing their own ideas and making sense out of their own experiences. It is also true because it is helpful to write about things you know about. When you write about things you know about, you can devote more of your energies to the writing itself and relatively less to research. Also, we tend to think more deeply and critically about things with which we are familiar. Everything else being equal, essays about the familiar may impress the instructor as more sophisticated than essays about unfamiliar topics.

With what in art are you familiar? If not the great monuments of the history of art, what of the architecture in your city, town, or campus? If not the paintings of the age of Baroque, what of the current cinema? Or what of the design of a coffeemaker or faucet? Or what of the "value" of all those Elvises on black velvet at the corner gas station on summer weekends?

WRITE ABOUT THINGS THAT INTEREST YOU

Another motive for writing is to help you learn and organize your thoughts about an interesting topic. Let's return to the obscenity issue. You may have strong ideas about nudity or obscenity, but little or no knowledge of the history of the issue or of the legal questions involved. Thus, you can focus on historic and legal issues as a way of expanding your knowledge of the subject.

Or consider issues such as Pop art and Conceptual art. You may have the feeling that these works are intriguing or perhaps that they are shams. What better way to

---

[3]Your professor's guidelines may differ somewhat, so it's a good idea to check. For example, some professors prefer that indented citations be single-spaced, whereas others insist that an entire paper be double-spaced.

become more conversant with them than to review the literature on them?

What if the instructor provides a list of topics and none of them interests you? For example, what if you must write a paper on some aspect of contemporary art but you have little interest in it. Perhaps you are interested in business and finance, in which case you could focus your paper on the collectors and the prices of contemporary art works. Or perhaps you are interested in poetry, in which case you could report on poetry about contemporary art. (Yes, it exists.)

Delimit the Topic

There is usually no magical fit between a topic and, say, a theme paper of 400 words or a term paper of 25 typewritten pages. By and large, you must make the topic fit. Believe it or not, it may be easier to blow up, or expand, an apparently small topic to term-paper size than to cut a broad topic down to size.

Are you interested in writing a theoretical paper on the "nature" of art? (If so, perhaps you should take out an insurance policy that protects you from sheer exhaustion.) As a first step, it would be wise to choose between a paper on art techniques (art fundamentals) or on the history of some aspect of art (perhaps an art movement, perhaps an artist). A historical paper on art techniques might be called something like "Development of Serigraphy" (silk-screen printing). Or you could write a paper on art fundamentals called "A Comparison of Oil and Acrylic Painting." Such a paper might examine the relative ease of working in these media and the quality of the outcomes. Rather than writing a paper called "History of Western Art," I would recommend focusing on, say, "The New York School in the 1950s" or "Postmodern Architecture of the 1980s." In either case, you could select a handful of renowned artists (or architects), recount criticisms of some of their works, include illustrations, and look for threads that seem to tie them into a movement.

Write a Thesis Statement

If you are writing an argumentative theme paper, it is helpful to clarify your purpose through a thesis statement. A thesis is a proposition that is maintained or defended in an argument. Once you have narrowed your topic, try to express the thesis of your paper as briefly as possible—in a single sentence, if you can. You don't have to include the thesis statement in your paper. Instead, you can pin it up on the wall and use it as a guide in writing. A thesis statement helps keep you from straying; it channels your arguments and evidence toward a goal.

Your paper "Postmodern Architecture of the 1980s" could be mainly descriptive or expository. On the other hand, you could express a thesis such as "Postmodern architecture is the humanization of technology."

Don't Wait for Inspiration—Get Going!

"Where shall I begin, please your Majesty?" he asked.

"Begin at the beginning," the King said, gravely, "and go on till you come to the end: then stop."

Lewis Carroll, *Alice in Wonderland*

The idea is to get the pencil moving quickly.

Bernard Malamud

The idea of getting going is not elementary or silly, even if it sounds so. Many students bog down soon after they select a topic. (So do many professional writers!)

Getting going can mean going to the library and beginning to research the topic. Getting going can mean making an outline. Getting going can mean following inspiration and jotting down the beginning of the paper, the conclusion,[4] or some of the ideas

---

[4]That's right! There's nothing wrong with writing down the conclusion of a paper, or the tentative conclusion of a paper, at the beginning. Just don't leave it there when you hand the paper in!

that you will probably use in the body of the paper. You can write down ideas on index cards or on loose-leaf pages that you reorder later on. If you are using word-processing, you can save random thoughts in separate files and integrate them later. You can also save them in the same file and then move them around as blocks of text later on.

The point is this: You've got to get going somewhere and at some time. If you have no plan at all, spend a few minutes to form-ulate a plan. If you have a plan and some useful thoughts come to you, feel free to stray from the plan and jot these thoughts down. It is easier to return to a plan than to reconstruct moments of inspiration!

For most of us, writing, like invention, is 10 percent inspiration and 90 percent perspiration. You cannot force inspiration. You can only set the stage for inspiration by delving into your topic—perhaps by formulating a plan (e.g., beginning with library work), perhaps by writing an outline, perhaps by talking with other people about the topic. Then, when inspiration strikes, jot it down. Keep this in mind, too: A good paper does not have to be inspired. A good paper can address the topic in a coherent, useful way without bursts of genius, without poetry.

Make an Outline

With nearly any kind of writing, it is helpful to make an outline. Short stories and novels profit from outlines of their plots and characters. Essays, even brief essays of the sort you may write on a test, profit from a listing of the issues to be raised or topics to be covered. With term papers, most students find it essential not only to list the topics that are to be covered, but also to sketch out how they will be covered.

Outlines usually take the following form:

   I.   Major head
      A. Second-level head
      B. Second-level head
        1. Third-level head
           (a) Fourth-level head

           (b) Fourth-level head
        2. Third-level head

Papers have beginnings (introductions), middles (bodies), and ends (conclusions). In writing theme papers and term papers, students can use a major head for the paper's introduction, one or more major heads for the body of the paper, and another major head for the conclusion.

Compose a Draft

A draft is a rough or preliminary sketch of a piece of writing. One way to write a draft of a theme paper or term paper is to flesh out an outline of the paper. Another is to start writing the sections you know most about, or have the strongest feelings about, and then assemble them like a puzzle. Still another is to just start writing, without even a mental outline, and somehow to arrive at what seems to be a completed work.

Let us assume that you are using an outline and consider how you might flesh it out, section by section.

INTRODUCTION TO THE PAPER

If you can't annoy somebody, there's little point in writing.

Kingsley Amis

The introduction has a number of func-tions, including arousal of reader interest, presentation of a number of the issues involved, and an explanation of what you will cover. You may want to include your thesis statement somewhere in the intro-duction (i.e., "It will be shown that. . ."), but it is not necessary. If you are going to wax poetic in a paper, the beginning is as good a place as any. Here are just a handful of the ways in which writers grab the reader's interest:

1. Using an anecdote (as concerning the antagonisms between Michelangelo and Pope Julius II).
2. Using an interesting piece of informa-tion from within the paper (e.g., "Shakespeare was born in the year that Michelangelo died").

3. Coupling a fact with irony (e.g., "Despite the argument that the Romans were mere imitators, they managed to create arches with two-ton blocks that have stood for 2,000 years, cemented together only by the force of gravity").
4. Using a quote (e.g., "How little there is that is classical in the spirit and even the form of the art of Donatello! How closely we have to scan the work or the utterances of Leonardo to find a trace of the study of Roman or Hellenic antiquity![5]).
5. Using a rhetorical question ("Did you know that a Volkswagen sports car is on display at the Museum of Modern Art?" or, "Did you know that `Barbarians' were responsible for the construction of our most magnificent cathedrals?" A so-called rhetorical question is not really meant to be answered, but is intended as an attention-grabbing way of leading into a topic.

You can also leave the writing of the important beginning lines of the paper until the end, when you have a greater grasp of the subject and are more acquainted with the issues involved. Of course, you are free to jot down notes about possible beginnings as you work on other parts of the paper—whenever inspiration strikes.

Then the introduction can go on to explain the issues that will be covered in the paper and how the paper will approach the topic.

BODY OF THE PAPER

The body of the paper is the meat of the paper. If you are criticizing a film, or an art exhibit, this is where you list the strengths and weaknesses of the work and support your views. If you are writing an argumentative theme, this is where you state your premises and explain your logic. If you are reviewing the research on dating ancient works of art, this is where you explain who did what, when, and how.

---

[5]Vasari, Giorgio. *Vasari on technique*. Trans. Louisa S. Maclehose (1960). New York: Dover Publications, p. 12.

CONCLUSION OF THE PAPER

The conclusion of a paper is a section that contains more than conclusions. Like the introduction, the conclusion has a number of functions.

The introduction of a paper tells readers where they're going. The conclusion tells readers where they've been. The first part of the concluding section is an excellent place for summarizing or briefly reviewing the information presented in the body. In the conclusion of a paper on feminist sculpture, you may want to summarize the features that make Maya Ying Lin's Vietnam Memorial (Fig. 6-7 in the text) a feminist monument. In summarizing the body, you are not simply adding words—that is, "padding" to meet a length requirement. You are reminding the reader of the major points as a way of leading up to your judgments, inferences, or opinions.

Then you may arrive at the conclusions themselves. Your conclusions put everything together. They explain what it all means. One conclusion of a paper on Pop art might be that some works show the "personal signature" of the artist, whereas others do not. You may even want to take a chance and attempt to categorize Pop art works in terms of approaches to brushwork and other features. You may want to take some kind of stand on the level of sophistication of ethnographic art, or arrive at criteria for determining when craft objects are to be considered works of fine art. Here you could also try a general statement about the frenetic or peripatetic editing techniques used in music videos.

Ideally, the conclusion section ends with a bang. The beginning of a paper may attempt to grab the reader's interest, and the ending sometimes also aims to achieve an impact. You can refer to future directions—perhaps the possibility that someday the computer may turn out more sophisticated works of art than Jean Tinguely's *Meta-matic No. 9* (Fig. 6-22 in the text). In a more matter-of-fact mode, you can suggest new avenues of research, new approaches to creating art, new forms of criticism. But you can also use humor, irony, or rhetorical

Overcoming a Writing Block

Ah, that blank sheet of paper! The possibilities are endless, so why can't you get something down?

All writers, not just college students, find themselves staring at that empty page now and then, wondering what they should do now. Everyone must occasionally cope with what writers refer to as "blocks."'

Here are some suggestions that may get you started if you are analyzing one or more works of art, as in a looking assignment:

1. Jot down some adjectives about the work or works. Don't be afraid to use simple, short words like "big" and "bright." Then see what follows.
2. Look for one or more dominant features in the work and begin to describe it. See what follows.
3. Jot down some interesting facts about the era in which the work was created. These can be historic facts—e.g., social or political—or art historical facts (concerning the development of style, polarities in style, matters of patronage, and so forth). Go from the era to the artist(s) or to the specific works.
4. List some interesting pieces of information about the artist(s). The information may relate to their family lives, their personal finances, their personalities, their circles of friends (and adversaries), and so forth. Go from the artist(s) to the era in general or to specific works.
5. Note some interesting critical commentaries about the artist(s) or the work(s). Go from there to the artist(s), to the work(s), or, perhaps, to the era.

What if you are stuck on a term paper? You have picked a topic and have gotten going on the paper, but now you have hit a wall. You have been staring at the page for half an hour, and nothing is coming to mind. What do you do now? Here are some additional ideas:

6. Brainstorm. In brainstorming, you do not try to narrow in on a single way to solve a problem. Instead, you generate as many kinds of approaches as possible. Set a time limit for your brainstorming. Then sit back and allow any relevant ideas to pop into mind, even outlandish ideas. Or ask roommates and friends for their ideas—even silly ones. During the session, just record ideas; don't judge them. When the session is finished, consider each idea and test those that seem most likely to be of help.

questions—the same devices that draw readers into papers.

The first few lines of the paper make your first impression. The last few lines make your final impression. These are the places where you want to make the greatest impact. If there are sentences you are going to work, work, and rework, let them be the first and last few sentences of the paper.

Revise the Paper

It's none of their business that you have to learn how to write. Let them think you were born that way.

Ernest Hemingway

I can't write five words but that I change seven.

Dorothy Parker

7. Take a break. Have a snack, call a friend, take a shower, get on the rowing machine. Then get back to work. You may find that your ideas have incubated while you were taking your break. Incubators warm chicken eggs so that they will hatch. In solving problems, including writing problems, incubation involves standing back from the problem for a while as we seem to continue to work on it at some level. Later on, a solution may appear to us as in a flash.

8. Work on another assignment. Instead of continuing to frustrate yourself, complete another assignment. Then return to the paper refreshed.

9. Force yourself to write. Make yourself write on the subject for a specific amount of time—say, for 20 minutes. Try to develop the arguments in the paper. Then critically examine what you have written.

10. Switch tools. If you've been processing words on a personal computer, try a typewriter for a while. Or use longhand.

11. Skip to another section. Work on another section of the paper. Type up the bibliography, for instance. (It's amazing how reviewing sources helps generate ideas!) Or work on your "dynamite" opening paragraph.

12. Let the paper go for a few days. This alternative may help when a short break is ineffective and you still have plenty of time to complete the paper. (Don't fall into the trap of kidding yourself about how much time remains!)

13. Check with the instructor. He or she may have some excellent advice for resuming the paper. Some instructors do not mind offering detailed suggestions.

14. Copy and go! Copy the last sentence or paragraph you wrote and just go with it! Or sketch four or five different directions you can take.

15. Accept reality? Sometimes you can't go on because your ideas are truly at a dead end. If the block persists, consider tossing out what you have written and starting from scratch. Perhaps you should change topics. If you have already written 20 pages or checked 50 sources, however, you may find it worthwhile to explore switching topics with your instructor before chucking it into the circular file (that is, the wastebasket).

Read over your compositions and, when you meet a passage which you think is particularly fine, strike it out.

Samuel Johnson

Wolfgang Amadeus Mozart is the great musician who bridged the Baroque and Romantic movements. His musical compositions are distinctive not only for their majesty, but also because they were composed practically without revision. It is as though his original conception of his music was complete and flawless. He is a rarity in the world of music.

It is also rare in the world of writing that our original ideas are complete and flawless. There are many false starts, many bad passages. Good writing usually requires revision, sometimes many revisions, even when the writer is experienced. Revision is a natural part of the writing process. Frequently, revision spells the difference between a paper that deserves an F and one that earns an A.

On the other hand, papers should not be revised just for the sake of revision. Now and then we may produce a first draft that we cannot improve. When this occurs, an old saying applies: "If it ain't broke, don't fix it."

There are revisions, and then there are revisions. Rarely is every sentence or even every section of a paper revised. Sometimes we revise papers in order to fine-tune our prose, to improve our sentence structure, to reconsider our choice of words. This type of revising is referred to as *editing*. Editing involves scrutinizing the paper word by word and changing anything that looks wrong, weak, or inappropriate. Editing extends to replacing words, sentences, and paragraphs with improved versions.

Sometimes we revise in order to reshape our ideas so that they fit together more coherently. At other times, we revise to fill gaps. At still other times, we labor to perfect our beginnings and endings.

How much revision is enough? That depends on you as a writer, on the piece that you are writing, and on the expectations of your instructors. As you move more deeply into your college career, you will gain a more accurate impression of how much revision your work usually requires to satisfy your professors—and yourself. Here are some specific suggestions for revising your papers:

1. *Create distance between you and your work.* Sometimes you need a bit of distance between yourself and your work to recognize weaknesses and errors. One good way to create this distance is to let time pass between drafts—at least a day. In this way, you may be able to look at certain passages or ideas from a new perspective. Of course, you cannot use this method if you don't begin a term paper until a few days before it is

due! Another method is to have a trusted friend, family member, or tutor at the college learning center look over the paper. Then you must try to listen to suggestions with an unbiased ear.

2. *Check the draft against the outline.* Are there obvious omissions? Have you strayed from the topic?

3. *Place earlier drafts beside you as you write.* Start writing from scratch, but follow the earlier versions as you proceed. Use segments of earlier versions that seem right. Omit sections that are weak or incorrect.

4. *Set aside earlier drafts and sketch a new version.* Then compare the sketch with earlier drafts, and incorporate the strengths of each version.

5. *Read the draft aloud.* When we listen to ourselves, we sometimes gain a new perspective on what we are saying— or not saying. This is another way to create a bit of distance between our writing and ourselves. You can also try reading the paper aloud to a friend.

6. *Try a new direction.* If something isn't working, consider taking a different approach. It is not unusual, for example, to change a thesis statement after completing a draft of a paper. Or you could find that you need to check out a different kind of research.

7. *Drop passages that do not work.* This may be the hardest piece of advice to follow. It is painful to throw a piece of work into the wastebasket, especially if we have devoted hours to it. Yet, not every effort is of high quality. *One of the important differences between artists and hacks is that the former are more willing to acknowledge their failures and to toss them onto the scrap heap.*

8. *Ask the instructor for advice.* Drop by during office hours and share some of your concerns with the instructor. You help organize your own thoughts and show respect for the instructor's time when you preplan your questions and make them fairly concrete.

Don't say, "I think something's wrong with my paper, but I don't know what." Say, instead, "My thesis was A, but the research seems to be showing B. Should I modify the thesis? Have I hit the right research?" By asking the instructor for advice, you do not appear weak and dependent. Instead, you appear sincere and interested in self-improvement. This is precisely the attitude that your instructor respects.

Proofread the Paper

A man occupied with public or other important business cannot, and need not, attend to spelling.

Napoleon Bonaparte

I know not, madam, that you have a right, upon moral principles, to make your readers suffer so much.

Samuel Johnson, letter to Mrs. Sheridan, after publication of her novel in 1763

This is the sort of English up with which I will not put.

Sir Winston Churchill

Napoleon was probably powerful enough, of course, that few would have brought misspellings to his attention. Most of us do not have the prerogatives of Napoleon. Proofreading is intended to catch the kinds of errors that make many professors groan and, in Johnson's words, "suffer so much." Proofreading is a form of editing directed at catching errors in spelling, usage, and punctuation, instead of enhancing the substance of the paper. Proofreading is not generally a creative process; it is more mechanical. On the other hand, if in proofreading you discover that a word does not accurately express your intended meaning, a bit of creativity might be needed in order to replace it or recast the sentence.

IMPORTANCE OF PROOFREADING

I will not go down to posterity talking bad grammar.

Benjamin Disraeli (Correcting one of his manuscripts on his deathbed)

For a largely mechanical process, proofreading is extremely important. For example, poor spelling and sentence structure suggest ignorance. Whether or not the instructor states that attention will be paid to spelling and so forth, you may still be judged by the mechanics. That is, an instructor who believes that you cannot spell may also believe that you cannot write a good paper.

When a paper has mechanical errors, the message to the instructor is very clear: You don't care enough to proofread the paper yourself or to have it proofread by someone who knows the mechanics.

Many campuses have tutorial centers at which you can have your papers proofread without charge. You may have a variety of reasons for not using the tutorial service: unwillingness to have your work scrutinized by someone else (but your instructor will scrutinize it, anyway); lack of time or inconvenient location (which is more inconvenient in the long run: writing the paper in time to have it proofread, or receiving a poorer grade than necessary?); or simply not caring. Whatever your reason, your instructor will interpret the flaws as signs of (1) lack of knowledge and (2) not caring—leading to lack of effort. Lack of knowledge and lack of effort are the two major reasons for poor grades on papers.

On the other hand, don't expect a proofreader to catch every error. Most tutors, for example, point out errors but do not make corrections themselves. Moreover, having a tutor check your paper does *not* remove your responsibility for catching and correcting errors. Nor does it guarantee that all errors have been highlighted. So don't blame your tutor for your own errors. The best way to work with a tutor is to have him or her read over your paper and make suggestions at various stages of the paper's development. You should also be striving to learn rules for proper usage—not just to catch the errors in a single paper.

TIPS FOR PROOFREADING

The following guidelines will help you proofread successfully:

1. When proofreading, read your paper letter by letter, word by word, phrase by phrase, punctuation mark by punctuation mark. (Some English professors recommend starting at the end of your paper and reading it backwards sentence by sentence as a way of catching small errors.) Don't focus on issues such as poetic value and persuasiveness of arguments. Pay attention to the littlest things. Are you using slang words to add color and help make your arguments, or are you just careless?

2. Check as to whether your tenses are consistent. Are you saying "Vasari *noted* (past tense) that . . ." in one place and "Vasari *argues* . . . (present tense)" in another?

3. Check whether subjects and verbs are in agreement. *Everyone* is a singular pronoun. Did you write "Everyone in *their* (plural) right mind. . ." when you should have written "Everyone in his or her right mind. . ."?

4. Check that sentences are, in fact, sentences, not fragments and not run-ons. If you're using sentence fragments here and there, be certain that they help highlight your points (e.g., "Not likely!") and do not reflect carelessness. Use fragments purposefully, not by accident.

5. Have a trusted friend proofread your papers in exchange for your proofreading the friend's. A page may look correct to you because you are used to looking at it. Errors might leap off the page upon perusal by someone else, however.

6. When in doubt, use a dictionary.

7. Check that your footnotes and bibliography contain the information required by your professor and are in the specified format.

8. Make certain that you have credited your sources so that you are not suspected or accused of plagiarism.

9. At the risk of being boring, I repeat: If the learning center at your college offers a proofreading service, use it.

PROOFREAD TO CORRECT COMMON WRITING ERRORS

Also proofread to correct common errors. Table 1 will alert you to a number of common errors in usage. Look for them as you proofread your paper. The table could have been endless; however, I chose to focus on some errors that are likely to make instructors think that students might be better off working in a car wash than taking a course in art.

Table 1:

Common Errors in English Usage and How to Correct Them.

Source of Confusion	Clarification
Confusing *accept* and *except*	*Accept* is a verb meaning "to receive favorably" or "to approve," as in "accepting someone's point of view." *Except* can be a verb, meaning "to leave out," or a preposition meaning "leaving out," as in, "They invited everyone except me."
Confusing *advice* and *advise*	*Advice* is a noun, something that is given, as in "This is my advice to you." *Advise* is a verb, meaning "to counsel" or "to give advice," as in "I would advise you to be cautious."
Confusing *affect* and *effect*	Most of the time, *affect* is a verb meaning "to stir or move the emotions" or "to influence." Consider this example: "I was affected by the movie." Most of the time, *effect* is a noun meaning "something brought about by a cause," as in the phrase

Produce the Final Copy

If you were applying for a job as a management trainee at a bank, would you show up in unwashed jeans and a T-shirt? (Rhetorical question.) I assume that you would want to make a good first impression, to look like a serious contender, to put your best foot forward. First impressions count with papers, too. You want your paper to look like a serious contender for an A.

Here are some guidelines for producing and packaging the final copy:

1. Consider buying a plastic or paper binder for your paper. Use a binder that's serious and professional looking, not frivolous. Stiff brown paper and clear plastic are superior, for example, to lavender-tinted plastic.

Table 1:

Common Errors in English Usage and How to Correct Them.

Source of Confusion	Clarification
	"cause and effect." Consider this example: "The movie had an enormous effect on me." *Affect* is also used as a noun, but usually only by mental-health workers. In that case, it is pronounced AF-fect and means "an emotion or emotional response." *Effect* is also occasionally used as a verb, meaning "to bring about or produce a result," as in "to effect change."
Confusing *affective* and *effective*	*Affective* is a word usually used only by psychologists or mental-health workers, meaning "of feelings" or "of emotions." Students are far more likely to use the word *effective*, meaning "having an effect" or "producing results." Consider this example: "Lisa made an effective speech."
Confusing *all right* and *alright*	Use *all right*. *Alright* is technically incorrect, and the Third College (1988) Edition of Webster's *New World Dictionary* (Simon & Schuster) lists "alright" as a variant spelling of "all right," whose usage is disputed. If your instructor marks "all right" wrong (which sometimes happens!), see him or her during office hours, pull out your dictionary, and be a hero. Be nice, not snide!
Confusing *allot, alot,* and *a lot*	Use *a lot* if you mean "many, plenty" or "a great deal." *Allot* (with two l's) is a verb meaning "to apportion" or "to distribute." There is no such word as. *alot.*
Confusing *all ready* and *already*	*All ready* means "Everyone" or "everything" is "ready," as in "We are all ready to get into the car," or "Dinner is all ready." *Already* means "done previously," as in "I wrote the paper already," or "The paper is already finished." *Already* can also be used at the end of a phrase to express impatience, as in "Stop it already!"
Confusing *allude, elude,* and *illude*	*Allude* means "to refer," as in "I alluded to Vasari's *On Technique* in my paper." *Elude* means "to avoid" or "to escape," as in, "He eluded the enemy." There is no such word as *illude*.

2. Follow the specified format exactly. For example, if your professor specifies margins of a certain width, stick to them like glue.
3. If your professor does not specify a format, ask about his or her preferences.
4. Include a cover page (unless instructed *not* to do so) with the following information:

Title of paper
Your name
Course title
Instructor's name
Date

5. *SPELL THE PROFESSOR'S NAME CORRECTLY.* You can find the proper spelling in the syllabus, college catalogue, or—usually—on the door of the professor's office.

Table 1:

Common Errors in English Usage and How to Correct Them.

Source of Confusion	Clarification
Confusing *allusion* and *illusion*	An *allusion* is a reference, as in "I made an allusion to Vasari's *On Technique.* An *illusion* is "a false idea or conception," or "a misleading appearance." Consider this example: "He used clothing to create the illusion that he was quite slender."
Confusing *all together* and *altogether*	*All together* means "all in the same place" or "all at once," as in, "Let's try singing that song again, all together this time." *Altogether* means "completely," as in "I'm altogether disgusted with the way you did that."
Confusing *among* and *between*	*Among* is used when there are three or more people or objects. *Between* is usually used when there are two people or objects. "We had $10 between us" and "Between you and me" is correct when two people are involved. "They distributed the money among us" is correct when three or more people have received the money.
Confusing *as* and *like*	As a preposition, *like* means "similar to" or "resembling," as in "The clouds look *like* cotton candy," or "This problem wasn't *like* the other problems." *As* usually means "to the same degree" ("The missile flew straight *as* a bullet") or "at the same time" ("He read *as* he watched TV").
Confusing *backward* and *backwards*	Use either one! They mean the same thing and are both acceptable.
Confusing *cite*, *sight*, and *site*	*Cite* is a verb usually meaning "to quote" or "to refer to," as in, "She *cited* the views of many experts in her argument." *Sight* is eyesight, or vision. A *site* is a piece of land, as in the "site of a work of architecture," or the place where something happens, as in "the site of a battle."
Confusing *data* and *datum*	*Data* is a plural noun, and *datum* is singular. A *datum* is a single piece of information, whereas the "data obtained in a study" usually refers to the entire mass of information assembled.
Confusing *etc.* and *et al.*	*Etc.* is the abbreviation of *et cetera* and means "and so forth." For example, "The company ran over budget on salaries, paper clips, coffee cups,

6. Learn the professor's preferred title (e.g., Ms., Dr.) and use it on the title page. A professor who has labored for many years to earn a doctorate may be justifiedly annoyed if you do not write "Dr." on the title page.

7. If the paper is a term paper, include a table of contents.

8. Use good-quality white paper. Do not use lined paper, onion-skin paper, or the cheapest quality ditto paper.

Table 1:

Common Errors in English Usage and How to Correct Them.

Source of Confusion	Clarification
	etc." *Et al.* is the abbreviation of *et alia*, meaning "and others." For most students, use of *et al.* is limited to lists of authors, as in, "In the study by Saeed et al., it was found that. . ." Note that *al* is followed by a period, whereas *et* is not.
Confusing *farther* and *further*	Today these words appear to be interchangeable, each one meaning "more distant or remote" or "additionally." *Farther* used to be limited in meaning to "more distant," however, as in, "They ran farther," and *further* used to be limited to "additionally," as in "They further investigated the issue." You will probably look more sophisticated if you stick to the older usage. You can pull out your dictionary if your instructor takes issue with your usage.
Confusing *flammable* and *inflammable*	Despite the fact that the prefix *in-* usually means "not," both words have the same meaning: "capable of catching on fire."
Confusing *have* and *of*	The confusion here usually occurs in contractions, such as *should've* or *could've*. When you can also use the verb *have*, use *'ve*, not the preposition *of*. Never write *could of, should of, would of*.
Confusing *I* and *me*	*I* is the subject of a verb, as in "*I* am going" or "She and *I* are going." *Me* is the object of a preposition, as in "Give it to her and (to) *me*," or the object of a verb, as in "Don't discourage John and *me*." Write "He and *I* gave books to charity," but write, "They threw the books at Jack and *me*."
Confusing *irregardless* and *regardless*	When in doubt, use *regardless*. *Irregardless* is nonstandard and technically incorrect.
Confusing *lie* and *lay*	This is where you make your mark! The verb *lie* means "recline," as in "*Lie* down" or "We have to *lie* low for a while." (*Lie* also means "to tell a lie.") The verb *lay* means "put or place down" and always takes a direct object, as in "*Lay* the book (direct object) on the table."
	The tenses of *lie* are as follows:
	Present tense: *Lie*, as in "I need to *lie* down," or "We intend to *lie* in wait right here."

9. Type your paper, double-spaced. (No excuses!)
10. Back in the days of the Model-T, it used to be said, "Make my car any color as long as it's black." Similarly, use any color of ink as long as it's black.
11. Make sure the ribbon is new or nearly new.

Table 1:

Common Errors in English Usage and How to Correct Them.

Source of Confusion	Clarification	
	Past tense:	*Lay*, as in "Earlier this morning I *lay* down for a while," or "This is where they *lay* in wait the other day.
	Past participle:	*Lain*, as in, "By the time dinner was ready, he had already *lain* down for a nap," or "They had *lain* in wait for six hours when the sun set.
	The tenses of lay are as follows:	
	Present tense:	*Lay*, as in "*Lay* down your weapons (objects)," or "Please *lay* the foundation (object) for the building."
	Past tense:	*Laid*," as in "They *laid* down their weapons," or "He *laid* the foundation for the building."
	Past participle:	*Laid*, as in "They had already *laid* down their weapons," or "By the time the carpenters were ready, the foundation for the building had been *laid*."
	Never, never (never) write or say "Lay down." Always use "Lie down."`	
Confusing *leave* and *let*	*Leave* can mean "to go away"; "to cause to stay," as in "*Leave* some food"; and "to bequeath," as in "*leaving* money to one's children or charity." *Let* usually means "to allow," as in "*Let* me go" or "*Let* it be."	
Confusing *lend* and *loan*	*Lend* is a verb and *lent* is the past tense, as in "She *lent* me some money yesterday." *Loan* is preferably used as a noun, as in "She gave me a small *loan*." There is no such word as *loaned*.	
Confusing *loose* and *lose*	Loose is an adjective, meaning the opposite of tight, as in "The knot came *loose*." *Lose* (pronounced *looz*) is the verb meaning "to misplace."	
Confusing *media* and *medium*	The noun *medium* is singular; *media* is plural. Television is a medium. Television, cinema, and photography are media.	

12. Try to use a standard pica or elite typeface, either 10 or 12 characters to the inch. If you're going to be creative, do so in your formation of ideas and in your masterly usage of the English language—not in your typeface. If you're using word processing and a printer, choose a letter-quality (or near-letter-quality) printer, not a dot matrix printer with annoyingly large dots.

Table 1:

Common Errors in English Usage and How to Correct Them.

Source of Confusion	Clarification
Confusing *ones* and *one's*	*Ones* is a plural noun, as in "This column contains four ones." *One's* is possessive, as in "It is good to do one's own work." *One's* is also the contraction of *one is*.
Confusing *phenomena* and *phenomenon*	*Phenomena* is the plural form of *phenomenon*.
Confusing *principal* and *principle*	A *principal* is an important or central person, as in "the principal museums of the United States." A *principle* is a guiding rule, such as Greek principle of the Golden Section.
Confusing *set* and *sit*	To *set* is "to arrange or put in place." Set takes a direct object, as in "*Set* the table (object)" or "*Set* the carton (object) down on the floor." To *sit* is "to be seated" or "to remain in place." Sit does not take a direct object, as in "Please *sit* down" or "The vase *sits* on the mantel."
Confusing *shall* and *will*	These auxiliary verbs are used to show future tense ("They *will* be ready tomorrow") or to express determination or obligation ("You *shall* do what I tell you to do!").

The formal approach of showing the future tense is as follows:

I shall go tomorrow
You will go tomorrow
He/she/it will go tomorrow
We shall go tomorrow
You (plural) will go tomorrow
They will go tomorrow

The formal approach to showing determination or obligation is as follows:

I will get this done
You shall get this done
He/she/it shall get this done
We will get this done
You (plural) shall get this done
They shall get this done

Your instructor may have other ideas. Why not stop by during office hours and ask about them?

13. Use margins of about an inch all around. Wider margins make a paper look skimpy. Narrower margins make a paper look cramped and hard to read. If you're using computer paper, carefully tear off the edges that contain the guiding holes.

14. Keep a copy of the paper. Professors may decide to hold on to some papers, and now and then a paper gets lost.

The rest is up to you.

Table 1:

Common Errors in English Usage and How to Correct Them.

Source of Confusion	Clarification
Confusing *stationary* and *stationery*	*Stationary* means "still" or "in one place," as in "A marble statue is a relatively stationary object." *Stationery* is what you write on—paper.
Confusing *taught* and *taut*	*Taught* is the past tense of teach. *Taut* means "tight," as in "The rope is taut."
Confusing *their*, *there*, and *they're*	*Their* is possessive, as in "They met *their* obligations." *There* shows location, as in "here and *there*." *They're* is the contraction of "they are."
Confusing *to*, *too*, and *two*	*To* is the preposition that shows location or destination, as in "Give the book *to* her" or "Go *to* school." *Too* is the adverb meaning "also," as in "I want to go, *too*," or "extremely," as in "That's *too* much!" *Two* is the number (2).
Confusing *toward* and *towards*	These prepositions have the same meaning and are both considered correct. I recommend using *toward* unless you are quoting someone's speech, in which case you would record what the person said or what you think the person would have said.
Confusing *use* and *utilize*	There is a slight difference in meaning between these words; to *utilize* is "to put to practical or profitable use." *Utilize* can make it seem that you're trying too hard, and you can't make a mistake if you stick to *use*. In short, use *use*. (Don't utilize *utilize*.)
Confusing *who* and *whom*	*Who* (or *whoever*) serves as the subject of a verb, as in "*Who* did this?!" *Whom* (or *whomever*) serves as the object of a preposition, as in "To (preposition) *whom* did you lend my car?" or as the object of a verb, as in "Choose (verb) *whomever* you prefer.
Confusing *whose* and *who's*	*Whose* is possessive, as in "*Whose* paper is this? It has no name!" *Who's* is the contraction of "who has" or "who is," as in the bear's lament, "*Who's* been sleeping in my bed?"
Confusing *your* and *you're*	*Your* is possessive, as in "This is *your* book." *You're* is the contraction of "you are," as in "I assume that *you're* going."

EXERCISE 1: UNDERSTANDING ART

"Everyone wants to understand art," wrote Pablo Picasso. "Why not try to understand the song of a bird? Why does one love the night, flowers, everything around one without trying to understand them? But in the case of a painting, people have to understand."

Is it possible to "understand" art, or is the endeavor an impossible quest? Is art subject to intellectual or rational analysis, or is it too esoteric and exotic to be comprehended in the way that scientific phenomena are comprehended? Why should we try to understand art? How can understanding art heighten our appreciation of art, or enhance the quality of life?

_____

_____

_____

_____

_____

_____

_____

_____

_____

_____

_____

_____

_____

_____

_____

_____

_____

EXERCISE 2: ART AND BEAUTY

Consider the following remarks about art:

"[Art] has as its foundation the beautiful, which is eternal and natural."

—Jean-Auguste-Dominique Ingres

"The artist . . . makes life more interesting or beautiful."

—George Bellows

"I believe in Michelangelo, Velasquez, and Rembrandt; in the might of design, the mystery of color, the redemption of all things by Beauty everlasting."

—George Bernard Shaw

What is the relationship between art and beauty? What is "beauty"? Is art by definition beautiful? Is the foundation of art "the beautiful"? Refer to works in the text in your response.

_____

_____

_____

_____

_____

_____

_____

_____

_____

_____

_____

_____

_____

_____

_____

_____

_____

_____

THINKING AND WRITING ABOUT ART

EXERCISE 3: ICONOGRAPHY

Iconography, as noted in the text, refers to the themes and symbols in works of art—themes and symbols that are connected with the meanings of the works.

Does knowledge of iconography contribute to one's appreciation of a work of art? Refer to works in the text to support your views. (Hint: Why not consider the role of colored light in a Gothic cathedral [Chapter 12]? Or what of Jan van Eyck's *Giovanni Arnolfini and His Bride* [Fig. 13-4]? Or Judith Shea's *Inaugural Ball* [Fig. 1-31]?)

_____

_____

_____

_____

_____

_____

_____

_____

_____

_____

_____

_____

_____

_____

_____

_____

_____

_____

_____

Name: _____   Date: _____

EXERCISE 4: COMPARE AND CONTRAST . . .

Compare and contrast Mondrian's *Composition with Red, Blue, and Yellow* with his *Broadway Boogie-Woogie*.

Piet Mondrian created numerous geometric abstract works, such as *Composition with Red, Blue, and Yellow* and *Broadway Boogie-Woogie*. How are they alike, and how do they differ? Both contain rectangles; both contain primary colors, albeit with very different visual impacts. Perhaps the key issue has to do with their titles. Hint: One of the works is nonobjective and the other is an abstraction of a pulsating metropolis. What do the titles suggest to you about the meanings of the works?

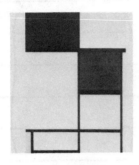

PIET MONDRIAN
Composition with Red, Blue, and Yellow

Courtesy Sidney Janis Gallery, N.Y.

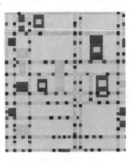

PIET MONDRIAN
Broadway Boogie-Woogie

1942-43
Oil on canvas, 50 x 50".
Collection, The Museum of Modern Art, New York.
Given anonymously.

_____

_____

_____

_____

_____

_____

_____

_____

_____

_____

_____

_____

_____

_____

EXERCISE 5: THE IMPORTANCE OF DRAWING TO THE ART OF PAINTING

Jean-Auguste-Dominique Ingres, the nineteenth century French painter, was also a magnificent draftsman. He wrote: "To draw does not simply mean to reproduce contours; drawing does not consist merely of line; drawing is also expression, the inner form, the plane, modeling. . . . Drawing includes three and a half quarters of the content of painting."

Now that you have read about drawing in Chapter 3 and Painting in Chapter 4, indicate whether or not you agree with Ingres's remarks. Refer to specific works in the text to support your views.

_____

_____

_____

_____

_____

_____

_____

_____

_____

_____

_____

_____

_____

_____

_____

_____

_____

_____

_____

EXERCISE 6: COMPARE AND CONTRAST . . .

Compare and contrast Gonzalez's *Woman Combing Her Hair* with Rodin's *The Walking Man*.

Compare and contrast the materials and styles of Gonzalez and Rodin as shown in these works. Is one realistic? Representational? Abstract? Nonobjective? Why or why not? Which is open form? Closed form? How does each artist manipulate his materials to create or evoke form? How do the artists penetrate or envelop the surrounding space in their compositions?

JULIO GONZALEZ
Woman Combing Her Hair

Moderna Museet, Stockholm.

AUGUSTE RODIN
The Walking Man

Bronze. 83 x 61 x 28 in. Photo by Lee Stalsworth Hirshhorn Museum and Sculpture Garden, Smithsonian Institution. Gift of Joseph H. Hirshhorn, 1966.

_____

_____

_____

_____

_____

_____

_____

_____

_____

_____

_____

_____

_____

_____

EXERCISE 7: ON TRUTHFULNESS TO MATERIALS

Contemporary sculptor Henry Moore argued that works of sculpture should be true to their materials: "Every material has its own individual qualities. . . . Stone, for example, is hard and should not be falsified to look like soft flesh."

How do sculptors take advantage of the properties of their materials or apparently contradict them? In your response, you may want to refer to the very different appearances that can be created by working with various materials—for example, blocky works in limestone (such as Bran-cusi's *The Kiss* [Fig. 1-47] versus some Renaissance or Baroque sculptures which falsify stone by their illusionistic realism (such as Bernini's *Apollo and Daphne* [Fig. 6-5]). You may wish to consider works such as Deborah Butterfield's *Horse #6-82* (Fig. 17-32) and Claes Oldenburg's *Soft Toilet* (Fig. 6-14). Can you think of any sculptures whose subjects seem almost oblivious to or outright contradict the qualities of the materials used by the artist, and whether or not this contradiction has a positive or negative effect on their artistic qualities?

_____

_____

_____

_____

_____

_____

_____

_____

_____

_____

_____

_____

_____

_____

_____

_____

_____

_____

EXERCISE 8: ON MAYA YING LIN'S VIETNAM MEMORIAL

Maya Ying Lin's Vietnam Memorial (Figure 6-7), in Washington, D.C., has been hailed by some critics as a feminist monument. How does Lin's memorial differ from standard heroic fare? (Consider the typical soldier on horseback, for example, the Roman triumphal arch, or the bronze sculpture (in Washington, D.C., of marines raising the U.S. flag on Iwo Jima.) What is the significance of the departure from the heroic? Describe the relationship of the viewer to each of these monuments. How do they differ?

_____

_____

_____

_____

_____

_____

_____

_____

_____

_____

_____

_____

_____

_____

_____

_____

_____

_____

_____

_____

EXERCISE 9: ARCHITECTURE AS A VEHICLE FOR ARTISTIC EXPRESSION

The text notes that "Architecture is . . . a vehicle for artistic expression in three dimensions."

Discuss architecture as an artform. Refer to works discussed in the text to compare architecture to other artforms, particularly sculpture. (You may wish to discuss Maya Ying Lin's Vietnam Memorial [Figure 6-7] and Eero Saarinen's TWA Terminal [Figures 7-23, 7-24] both as sculptures and works of architecture.) What unique opportunities (and limitations) for artistic expression are encountered by architects? (Hint: In your response, you may wish to refer to the types of compromises architects must make.)

_____

_____

_____

_____

_____

_____

_____

_____

_____

_____

_____

_____

_____

_____

_____

_____

_____

_____

EXERCISE 10: ARCHITECTURE IN ITS CULTURAL SETTING

Throughout the text, it is noted that the arts of an age express the values of that age and various aspects of the technology of the age. Show how various examples of architecture reflect the practical needs, values, aesthetics, and technologies of the cultures and societies in which they were created. In your discussion, you may wish to refer to works as diverse as the pre-Columbian "cliff palace" in present-day Colorado, the cathedrals of the Middle Ages, the houses in Levittown, examples of steel-cage architecture, and works of the Postmodern movement.

_____

_____

_____

_____

_____

_____

_____

_____

_____

_____

_____

_____

_____

_____

_____

_____

_____

_____

_____

_____

EXERCISE 11: ARCHITECTURE IN ITS SITE

In designing buildings, architects must not only be sensitive to the aesthetics of their structures, but must pay attention to the relationships between them and their sites. Sites include not only the natural environment, but also neighboring buildings and, sometimes, existing structures to which new ones will be connected (especially in the case of architectural additions).

Show how a number of the architectural works discussed in the text are integrated with (or antagonistic to) their sites. You may find it particularly stimulating to consider works such as Maya Ying Lin's Vietnam Memorial (Figure 6-7), Mies van der Rohe's Farnsworth House (Figure 7-20), I. M. Pei's addition to the Louvre (Figure 7-12), and Williamson Hall at the University of Minnesota (Figure 7-31).

_____

_____

_____

_____

_____

_____

_____

_____

_____

_____

_____

_____

_____

_____

_____

_____

_____

_____

EXERCISE 12: PHOTOGRAPHY AS THE GREAT EQUALIZER

Photography has been referred to as a great equalizer or a great "democratizer." Photography, that is, makes it possible for almost anyone to capture reality on a two-dimensional surface, or create a work of visual interest. It also makes it possible for nearly anyone to have portraits of themselves and their families. Prior to the advent of photography, this was a luxury afforded by those who could commission an artist to render their likeness.

Discuss the role of photography as a medium that enhances the average person's connection to the visual arts.

_____

_____

_____

_____

_____

_____

_____

_____

_____

_____

_____

_____

_____

_____

_____

_____

_____

_____

_____

_____

EXERCISE 13: PHOTOGRAPHY VERSUS PAINTING

"Photography," wrote Edward Weston, "has or will eventually negate much of painting—for which the painter should be deeply grateful; relieving him, as it were, from certain public demands (such as) representation, objective seeing."

Has photography "negated" certain styles of drawing and painting? Which ones? Is there little purpose to artists' continuing to draw or paint in a manner that reproduces reality? In your response, you may wish to refer to works as diverse as Jan van Eyck's *Giovanni Arnolfini and His Bride* (Figure 1-52), John Singer Sargent's *Madame X* (Figure 9-32), Elizabeth Murphy's *Self-Portrait with Pansy* (Figure 2-48) or Richard Estes's *Helene's Florist* (Figure 17-20).

_____

_____

_____

_____

_____

_____

_____

_____

_____

_____

_____

_____

_____

_____

_____

_____

_____

EXERCISE 14: THE PHOTOGRAPHY OF ROBERT MAPPLETHORPE

Mapplethorpe, who recently died of AIDS, was the center of hotly debated issues concerning the borders between art and obscenity. Some of his works portrayed men in homosexual acts and nude children (the children were not involved in sexual activity). You may recall that the city of Cincinnati lost an obscenity case against a gallery that showed many of his photographs.

Others of his photographs, such as *Ajitto (Back)*, shown here, reveal Mapplethorpe's interest in the male form but are not sexually suggestive. In this exercise, compare and contrast *Ajitto* with Edward Weston's photograph *Pepper No. 30* (Fig. 1-37). (Hint: Reread Chapter 1's description of the Weston photograph.) Since they are both studies in form, discuss their visual similarities and formal qualities. Does the knowledge of obscenity issues bias your appreciation of *Ajitto* on a formal level?

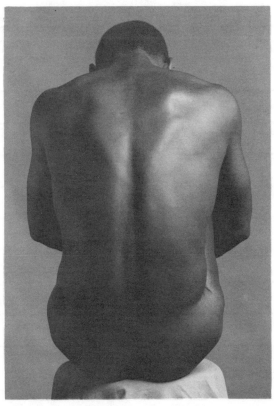

ROBERT MAPPLETHORPE
Ajitto (Back)

© 1981 The Estate of Robert Mapplethorpe

_____

_____

_____

_____

_____

_____

_____

_____

_____

_____

EXERCISE 15: CINEMATOGRAPHIC TECHNIQUES

In addition to story lines, actors, and sets, cinematography and video use various techniques to achieve their impacts. Slow motion, panning, narrative and parallel editing, close-ups and longshots, flashbacks and flashforwards, fading, color, animation, and special effects are but a few.

Compare and contrast two works from the same medium (e.g., film, music video, etc.). Show how one uses several of these techniques to achieve its effect on the audience, whereas the other relies more on the story line and, perhaps, the music.

_____

_____

_____

_____

_____

_____

_____

_____

_____

_____

_____

_____

_____

_____

_____

_____

_____

_____

_____

EXERCISE 16: THE LINE BETWEEN CRAFTS AND FINE ART

According to the text, Robert Arneson's *Jackson Pollock* (Fig. 9-5) "illustrates how blurred the line between craft and fine art can be." Where do crafts end and fine arts begin? Which objects in Chapter 9 impress you as fine art? Why? As you leaf through the textbook, can you find illustrations of any other objects which seem to blur the distinction between craft and fine art? Why, in these cases, is the distinction unclear? Should a distinction be made at all?

_____

_____

_____

_____

_____

_____

_____

_____

_____

_____

_____

_____

_____

_____

_____

_____

_____

_____

_____

_____

EXERCISE 17: ON ALL THE PARTHENONS

The text notes that the Parthenon (Figure 11-8, page 270) has been one of the most influential buildings in the history of architecture. Consider the text's illustration of the Parthenon, and look for illustrations of the Parthenon in other books in your library. Now go on a walking tour through your city, town, or campus. (If your professor agrees that your location makes this unfeasible, consider books in your library that have photographs of buildings in American cities, or check the travel section in a local bookstore for such books.) List a number of buildings that appear to have been influenced by the Parthenon, and indicate how each one adapts elements of their classical Greek prototype.

_____

_____

_____

_____

_____

_____

_____

_____

_____

_____

_____

_____

_____

_____

_____

_____

_____

_____

_____

_____

EXERCISE 18: ILL-GOTTEN ART

The text notes that the Euphronious vase, or calyx krater (Fig. 11-12), in the collection of New York's Metropolitan Museum of Art may have been illegally sold by grave robbers to an American who, in turn, smuggled the vase out of Italy and sold it to the museum of Art for $1 million.

The vessel is only one example of works of art that have been removed throughout history from their countries of origin by individuals as diverse as archaeologists and conquerors, army privates and private collectors, grave robbers and ambassadors. Thomas Hoving, director of the Met when the Krater was purchased, dismissed the controversy as "a lot of hot air" and noted that the calyx krater was declared when it came into the United States, so it was here legally.

Is it sufficient that this and other works acquired under similar circumstances are in the United States (or other countries other than the country of origin) "legally"? To whom do such works belong? To private parties in, or the governments of, countries where investors have paid for them, or their countries of origin? If they were considered the property of their countries of origin, what would be the effects on the world of art?

_____

_____

_____

_____

_____

_____

_____

_____

_____

_____

_____

_____

_____

_____

_____

EXERCISE 19: COMPARE AND CONTRAST . .

Compare and contrast Savoldo's *St. Matthew* with Two Carolingian *St. Matthews*.

The St. Matthews on p. 304 of your textbook provide a remarkable study in contrast. One is classical and scholarly, the other is frenetically secretarial, as though he were a dutiful conduit between God and the written word. Savoldo's *St. Matthew*, painted about 700 years later, is almost mystical by contrast, front-lit, as he is, by a small flame. St. Matthew leans back from his manuscript into the darkness, where an angel whispers to him. People in the background suggest that he has stolen away to a hidden chamber to seek divine inspiration. What do the three St. Matthews suggest about each artist's views of the relationship between God and humanity? How does each artist use lighting, brushwork, figure, and background to express his concept?

SAVOLDO
St. Matthew

Oil on Canvas. H. 36-3/4 in. W. 49 in.
The Metropolitan Museum of Art, Marquand Fund, 1912

_____

_____

_____

_____

_____

_____

_____

_____

_____

_____

_____

_____

_____

_____

EXERCISE 20: ON THE RENAISSANCE

The word *Renaissance* means "rebirth." Refer to specific Renaissance artists and works to illustrate just *what* was reborn during the Renaissance. You may also wish to include works by thinkers, philosophers, writers, or architects in your essay.

_____

_____

_____

_____

_____

_____

_____

_____

_____

_____

_____

_____

_____

_____

_____

_____

_____

_____

_____

_____

_____

_____

_____

_____

EXERCISE 21: COMPARE AND CONTRAST . . .

Compare and contrast Clouet's *Francis I* with Leonardo's *Mona Lisa*. How does each artist model the figure? Who uses chiaroscuro? Who relies on line to create a sense of form? Which pose is more natural? Which is more stilted? Why? Who suggests depth? Who compresses space? How? Which portrait is more psychologically revealing? Why?

JEAN CLOUET
Francis I
Scala/Art Resource

LEONARDO DA VINCI
Mona Lisa
Giraudon/Art Resource

_____

_____

_____

_____

_____

_____

_____

_____

_____

_____

_____

_____

_____

_____

_____

EXERCISE 22: DAVID, DAVID, DAVID, AND . . . DAVID

The Renaissance and the age of Baroque can boast of the production of many remarkable *Davids*, four of which are illustrated in your textbook: Those of Donatello, Verrocchio, Michelangelo, and Bernini. Compare and contrast these works, attending to style, technique, the physical attributes of each David, and the moment depicted in each sculpture.

_____

_____

_____

_____

_____

_____

_____

_____

_____

_____

_____

_____

_____

_____

_____

_____

_____

_____

_____

EXERCISE 23: STYLISTIC POLARITIES

When we think back on various periods in the history of art, we note that periodically, a polarity of style has existed between the intellectual and the emotional. Describe this stylistic polarity in the following periods: Hellenistic Greece, the age of Baroque, the early Nineteenth Century (Neoclassicism and Romanticism), and the Post-Impressionist era, and the early Twentieth Century. Refer to specific artists and works of art to illustrate these contrasting styles (such as Matisse's *The Green Stripe* and Picasso's *Seated Woman*).

_____

_____

_____

_____

_____

_____

_____

_____

_____

_____

_____

_____

_____

_____

_____

_____

_____

_____

_____

_____

EXERCISE 24: MUST ARTISTS PERSONALLY EXECUTE THE PHYSICAL EMBODIMENTS OF THEIR ARTISTIC CONCEPTS?

"A rose by any other name may smell as sweet," notes the text, "but would a Rubens painted by any other artist still be a Rubens?" Rubens was not only an artist; he was also a businessman who ran a workshop and employed assistants to work on his paintings to meet the demands of his patrons. Similarly, the heavy steel sculptures of some contemporary artists have been crafted by factory workers according to the artists' blueprints. Moreover, many printmakers have assistants or technicians do the actual printing of their works.

Respond to some of the questions raised in the text about such delegation of responsibility in works of art. For example, which is more essential to a work of art—its conception or its execution? Consider works of various media—drawing, painting, sculpture, and architecture. Refer to specific works from a variety of periods to consider, in each case, the extent to which the artist should also be the technician.

_____

_____

_____

_____

_____

_____

_____

_____

_____

_____

_____

_____

_____

_____

_____

EXERCISE 25: COMPARE AND CONTRAST . . .

Compare and contrast Caravaggio's *Judith and Holofernes* with Gentileschi's *Judith Decapitating Holofernes*.

The canvases by Gentileschi (see p. 365) and Caravaggio were painted during the same era. How are they both prime examples of the Baroque style? Consider the lighting, the palette, the brushwork, and the "stop-action" technique in your answer.

The subject matter is also the same. All these constants afford us the opportunity to focus on individual expression. One painting is by a woman artist, the other by a man. Is it obvious which is which? Why? Caravaggio depicts Judith as a fair young woman who is repulsed by the deed. How does Gentileschi's approach differ?

CARAVAGGIO
Judith and Holofernes

Scala/Art Resource

ARTEMISIA GENTILESCHI
Judith Decapitating Holofernes

Scala/Art Resource

_____

_____

_____

_____

_____

_____

_____

_____

_____

_____

_____

_____

_____

THINKING AND WRITING ABOUT ART

EXERCISE 26: WHAT IS MODERN ABOUT MODERN ART?

"Just what is modern about modern art?" asks the text. Compare and contrast some of the paintings in Chapter 15 (Modern Art) with those of Chapters 13 and/or 14 to develop your answers to this question. In your response, you may wish to spend some time discussing changes in the concept of pictorial space that emerged with the birth of modern art.

_____

_____

_____

_____

_____

_____

_____

_____

_____

_____

_____

_____

_____

_____

_____

_____

_____

_____

_____

_____

_____

EXERCISE 27: CHANGES IN THE CONCEPT OF PICTORIAL SPACE

Follow examples of changes in pictorial space by considering works in your textbook by the following artists: The mosaic artist of *Justinian and His Attendants*, Leonardo da Vinci, Pietro da Cortona, Jacques-Louis David, Paul Cézanne, Pablo Picasso, and Piet Mondrian.

_____

_____

_____

_____

_____

_____

_____

_____

_____

_____

_____

_____

_____

_____

_____

_____

_____

_____

_____

_____

_____